The

FRIED EGG ANALOGY

Eliminate

Lost Productivity

Caused By Meetings

by

JAMES FROST

Edition 1

First Published in November 2024

ISBN: 9798345618752

Disclaimer – The ideas and recommendations presented in this book are based on the author's own experiences and no guarantees are given regarding their validity, applicability or results when undertaken by the reader in his/her own circumstances.

Author's website: www.sjfacilitation.com

Dedication

This book is dedicated to the thousands of people with whom I've shared a meeting room over the past 40 years.

Contents

Meetings, Meetings and More Meetings

Apparently, over the last 20 years or so, the number of meetings we hold has been increasing by around 10% every year, and the trend looks to continue. That means where we would have one meeting in 2004, we now have six!

In most organizations, the higher you go up the hierarchical ladder, the more time you tend to spend in meetings. Middle management typically spend some 35% of their time in meetings, whilst senior executives will spend much more. A general average for office-based employees seems to be around 15-25%, but this obviously depends very much on the nature of the business. Whatever it is, it's a significant amount of employee time.

If you go onto the internet and search for meeting statistics, you'll find a great deal of information. A lot of the stats that come up are quite alarming and tend to focus on the *negative* aspects of meetings, mainly because the information comes from companies whose products aim to solve some of the problems they illustrate. Nevertheless, some are quite shocking.

One very interesting site* states that in an employee survey, almost 50% of the respondents said that meetings are the single biggest timewaster at work. A similar percentage admitted to being overwhelmed by the number of meetings and videoconferences they must attend per week.

How do these findings sit with you?

How about that weekly progress meeting, full of repetition, with things being discussed that don't concern you?

Or the meeting with too many topics to discuss properly in the time available?

Or spending hours preparing a meeting that then lasts less than an hour with no real outcome?

Or doing other things in a meeting, because the actual topic is not that critical to you, and you're desperate for the meeting to finish to get on with your own stuff?

Does any of this sound familiar?

All these are symptoms of under-productive meetings, and being under-productive implies wasted resources. In other words, a cost. Accumulated costs of un-productive meetings can be astronomical, running into the hundreds of billions of dollars of losses per year for businesses on the global scale.

Meetings are, however, an essential element of business life, and to which most of us dedicate a considerable portion of our work time. Not only are they one of the **most critical** elements of work, but, when you consider the time spent in them, for many of us they can be one of the **most dominant** aspects of our work life.

Love them or hate them, we are always going to be having meetings, due to the good and necessary outputs from collective action and thinking, even though it's widely accepted that some aspects of our meetings culture are not always positive.

This topic of meetings has produced over the years thousands of articles, studies, surveys, books, courses and more lately IT platforms, all of which attempt to address the issue of the deficiencies of meetings and how to improve them.

So, what's different about this book?

Basically, it looks at meetings from a different perspective via a simple illustration which I call the **Fried Egg Analogy**. I think it is applicable to pretty much any organization and highlights the need to understand what meetings are for in terms of *value,* both for the employees who participate and for the company.

This book has a clear objective, and that is to convince the reader, wherever they may sit in their organization, going from the most junior to the top-level executive, that no matter how good you think your meeting culture is, not to underestimate or ignore the cumulative effects of the meetings your organization holds.

*Source:

https://www.booqed.com/blog/minutes-wasted-of-meeting-50-shocking-meeting-statistics

Introduction

I first drafted this text during my last year of full-time employment, but several years have gone by before finalizing and publishing it. Even after this hiatus, the memories of corporate life linger on, and I can honestly say that I do not miss meetings in the slightest.

The reason being that, if you asked me in general terms over my career, what percentage of meetings I would have considered as great, enjoyable, productive, or even motivating, if I were to be brutally honest, I'd have to say less than 10%!

I've been in thousands of meetings. In my earliest years, the internet, mobile phones, personal computers, Powerpoint, projectors, video links...none of these existed. Not even calculators! I mention this not to reveal how old I am, but to underline my journey in having seen how the evolution of technology and cultural change has impacted and influenced how business is done, and more specifically the evolution of meetings over the years.

I mentioned culture, because people are still the most important component of a meetings' success or failure. Whilst technology has brought so much change, it is still *people* who are the major factor in business, how they are trained and educated, how they behave and speak, the relationships and hierarchical rules that they follow. The in-house cultures of today's companies are quite different from what they used to be.

Whist the advances in technology have dramatically affected the way we do business over the last 50 years, I have no doubt that the changes that will arise from the mainstream introduction of Artificial Intelligence will be as dramatic, if not more so. But that's another topic for another day!

In my thousands of meetings, I've seen and heard brilliant people, destructive people, aggressive people, respectful as well as disrespectful people. I've fallen asleep in meetings (who hasn't?). I've been exasperated, I've seen shouting matches even to the point of physical confrontation, I've seen clashes of cultures, I've endured the endless storytelling of the "never-shuts-up" monologue, I've been in meetings running past mid-night, I've seen meetings hijacked by clever talkers, meetings where everyone is terrified by the boss from hell, and nobody says a word. I've been invited to meetings having no idea why I am there, I've been in meetings where I didn't understand the language and I've facilitated hundreds of meetings in more than one language.

In a nutshell, when it comes to meetings, I think I've seen it all, and am acutely aware of the implications of meetings, both the good and the bad.

During the later years of my career, the number of meetings in which I had to participate had become crippling - a minimum of two to three each day, sometimes more. On top of this, the amount of information I was being confronted with daily when I switched on my computer screen in the morning, was simply overwhelming. There were systems for this, systems for that, news feeds, emails, collaborative team sites, reports, information management sites, human resources systems.... the list goes on.

I am sure the younger folks of today's labour market tackle such excesses of information with much more ability than I managed, but I do know that almost everyone I discuss the topic with (then and now) agree that the number of meetings and information overload are a challenge.

I'll also take a moment to admit that I was never very good in meetings!

You might find that admission curious, as I'm writing a book on the subject, but things like clarity and authority of speech, personality "presence", the ability to convince an audience through words, fast debating reaction times and memory of key data and facts were never my forte, often compounded by language limitations.

I remember many of the meeting "stars" I shared meetings with over the years; those folks who seemed to thrive in meetings, dominate meetings, drive meetings. They had all these competencies I have just mentioned. The Meeting X-Factor.

I remember meetings always seemed to be dominated by one or two people, many times the boss being one of them, which comes as no surprise. There always appeared to be in imbalance in contribution from the different people round the table, and many were the times that the only way you could get a word in was to shout someone else down.

In the early days, I would sit in meetings with ideas in my head that I didn't seem to be able to get out, wondering, as the meeting progressed at the pace and direction of the "drivers" why myself and others like me seemed to be just along for the ride rather than being equally proactive participants.

I often considered meetings as stages for people to compete and show how they are the smartest in the room. Even back then, I recognised this to be a serious deficiency of poorly managed meetings as it was clearly a personality and team-management issue. Obviously, with seniority and experience came more confidence and my ability to influence.

Reliable and smart videoconferencing has gained in popularity over the last 20 years, with the Covid pandemic and the working from home boom giving it a massive impulse. Today, videoconferencing has become as common as face-to-face meetings. In fact, hybrid meetings, where one or more participants are connected remotely, is now very much the norm, and some of the 360-degree audio-visual technologies now available are making virtual meetings very close to the face-to-face experience.

Remote working has increased the number of meetings we hold, in part because being physically separated from your organization can give an increased "need to connect" via a virtual meeting. In the old office environment, many of these meetings might have been simply an impromptu chat by the coffee-machine, but now they are more formal "scheduled" meetings, using collaborative platforms to facilitate the scheduling and execution.

These platforms also offer more than just meeting the planning and execution tools. They also handle integration of data, day-to-day communications (which sometimes duplicates other channels), and all sorts of intelligent tools for remote and collaborative team working, all of which intend to enhance the collaboration experience and process.

Along with the evolution of the corporate culture, another aspect of business that I can clearly identify as having changed dramatically over the years, and which I believe is most definitely linked to the issue of meetings, is that of individual responsibility and task.

At the beginning of my career there seemed to be a lot less "collaboration" and more individual responsibility, whereas today, teaming, collaboration and shared activities on a continual basis are very much the norm.

Whilst it is not within the scope of this book to get into the merits of this transformation nor the growth in teamwork, one thing I'll bet my hat on is that this transformation has created more meetings!

As I said, I first drafted this book whilst in full-time employment, so convinced was I of the growing problem. Our organization was frequently under tremendous project pressure timelines, with people often working late into the night, and the amount of time being spent in meetings was simply getting out of hand. Something had to be done and not surprisingly, when trying to raise cross-departmental or hierarchically vertical discussion on the subject of revising our meeting culture, there seemed to be very little appetite for addressing the issue; everyone was too busy...in meetings!

I mentioned the issue of information overload. Switching on the computer screen in the morning, and being overwhelmed by the sheer amount of information, communications, news, links, requests, and yes, meeting invites I was faced with daily.

With time, I became numbed and began filtering automatically the most important information from the rest, which often wound up being completely ignored. I simply didn't have time nor the mental capacity to address everything.

With respect to the meeting invites that popped up daily, each one required immediate analysis. What's it for? Why am I being invited? Do I have to attend? Do I have a schedule clash? What will I have to do to prepare? Do I accept now? All this took time and brainpower. And that was just for accepting the meeting invite!

Regarding the meetings I wanted to convene myself, there were the usual preparatory tasks. Who to invite, the need to check everyone's availability through shared calendars, prepare pre-read information, prepare the meeting and the PowerPoint!

I will not get into the pros and cons of PowerPoint, save to say that, in my opinion, it has been one of the most *destructive* as well as one of the most *constructive* tools to affect business productivity since the introduction of the desktop!

Anyway, point made. We have lots of meetings. Good and bad. Productive and not so productive.

About this book

The intention is that it should take the reader around 45 minutes to read this book; slightly more than the average meeting duration.

I've listed the main conclusions in the final chapter as a wrap-up.

It's also worth mentioning that whilst the principal target audience of this book is those who work in the larger companies, with hundreds or even thousands of employees, even if you are not part of such a large organization, meetings can still be massively destructive.

For example, having to travel across town to a certain venue, like someone else's office, only to have a fruitless meeting, meaning you've lost the whole morning, and when there are not many of you in your organization, can be a massive hit on your week.

Or perhaps attending a meeting where more questions arise than are answered, meaning the net result will be yet another meeting? And as we'll see later, it's not only simply about lost time. There are other intangible dangers arising from poor meeting culture.

Just because you don't have that many meetings either yourself or in your organization, doesn't necessarily mean you don't have some of the non-productivity issues more commonly associated to the larger companies.

Whatever the size of your organization, just ask yourself a couple of quick questions.

a) What percentage of the meetings I attend are less than optimally productive for me when I consider the whole "before, during and after" aspects related to those meetings (time, preparation, travel, cost, quality of outputs, etc)?

b) What percentage of the meetings I attend are less than optimally productive for all those who participate, considering all the "before, during and after" aspects?

You'll probably have a "feeling" of where you stand, but most likely nothing more than that. Nothing quantifiable.

So, whatever your business environment, you will be having meetings which will be taking up a considerable amount of time and resources both for yourself and your colleagues. In these times of expensive or scarce resources, and bottom-line pressures, if you don't know how your meeting culture is in terms of productivity and value, you are probably disregarding the health of one of the most important aspects of business life.

I'll now take a moment for a bit of framing and definition.

Taking a dictionary definition of the MEETING as:

"An assembly of people for a particular purpose, especially for formal discussion",

this book will be focussed mainly on meetings of more than two people but limited to up to a maximum of 10-15 people.

I will not be addressing large-scale workshops or conferences, and I will try to keep things general enough such that they apply to presential meetings, Videoconferences and hybrid meetings, the last two of which probably now make up the majority of meetings.

I also think it necessary to make a few clear statements from the outset:

- Meetings and teamwork are essential and always will be, and I am a firm supporter of holding good meetings.

- All companies are different and will have their own unique "cultures" and methodologies. Some manage things very well, some not so well. The question is, do you know where you stand?

- People at all levels call for meetings, for the different reasons they may have. Managers tend to call for more meetings than junior employees. But, when someone convenes a meeting, just how conscious are they of the impact in terms of cost/benefit their meeting will have on the invitees?

- There are companies, and there are cultures, that are more "disciplined" than others regarding meeting management, participation and execution. (Maybe it's to do with the sun, but in my experience, the warmer the climate, the more emotive and less-structured things tend to get!).

- Technology, and particularly collaborative and information-sharing platforms bring tremendous benefits to the whole process of meetings. But they also have their own inherent dangers, and their value should not be assumed or go un-checked.

- This book does not provide specific solutions to improve a company's meeting culture. As said, all companies are different, use different information systems and collaborative platforms, have different protocols and it is therefore impossible to propose one solution for all.

Finally, I'll re-state the principal objective of this book, which is to persuade you to stop ignoring the elephant in the room and convince yourself that maybe you should just take a bit of time to ask some questions in your organization about how you are doing regarding your meeting culture.

The implications can be enormous.

Billions of Dollars In Lost Productivity

Let's consider one of those alarming statistics mentioned in the first chapter. The billions of dollars of losses in productivity due to the non-productive aspects of meetings. How on earth do such dramatic numbers arise?

I'll give you a simple real-life exercise, which I think will serve to illustrate the problem.

A company had recently relocated its head office to a new premises, a campus-style office complex housing all business units. There were some three thousand employees in total on the campus, housed in four separate buildings, which were arranged around a central open-air recreation area. The new, interior design in each building also incorporated the concept of the "open space" working environment, whereby individual offices were for only the highest of management. Everyone else worked in open, shared spaces.

Each floor contained an assortment of glass-walled meeting rooms, ranging from the 2-3 person "pods" up to the larger, more traditional meeting room for 10-15 people. Reservation of a meeting room was done via an online booking platform, with a smart screen outside each room indicating who the reservation was made by or for, and the duration of the booking. The larger rooms had all the usual latest technology communications, video, projection and IT facilities.

What was very apparent was the difficulty in reserving a meeting room, such was the demand. To get a room for an urgent meeting was virtually impossible, as all rooms were pretty much booked up all day, every day.

So, let's make a quick back-of-the-envelope calculation for the building.

There were 4 floors in the building, with 10 meeting rooms per floor. That's 40 rooms. Some big, some small. Let's say for the sake of this exercise, the rooms were booked up for 70% of each day (it was probably more like 100%, but let's not be extreme!) and each meeting lasted an hour on average, with 5 participants in each (presential, virtual or hybrid).

Assuming there are 22 working days in a month, the maths gives:

40 rooms x 1 hr x 5 people x 8 hrs in a day x 70% usage x 22 days

= **_24,640 employee-hours_** in meetings in any one month

That's 3,080 employee-days dedicated full-time to meetings in a month, or the equivalent of **_140 employees being full-time, all day, every day of the month, in meetings_**.

Note that this estimation does not consider the number of employees in the building – it's simply based on meeting room usage.

Now, here's the interesting part.

Let's say that the **average productivity** of the participants in each meeting is **60%.** By this, I mean one of two things:

- For **60% of the time in the meeting, all participants are fully engaged** and adding maximum value to themselves and the company. For the other 40% of the time, they're less than fully productive, like being distracted by their phones, thinking they should be elsewhere, thinking about other stuff they have to do, trying to multi-task and work on some other issue, even daydreaming.

or

- During the meeting, **60% of the participants are fully engaged 100% of the time,** with the other 40% being in a less productive mode.

So, what does this mean for our meeting room scenario? We calculated the equivalent of 140 employees full time, all day every day in meetings, so, if the average meeting productivity is only 60%, then we have the equivalent of **56 employees being under-productive, all day, every day** throughout the month due to these meetings. That's a lot of people.

Now, you can argue the numbers, especially the productivity estimates, but this hypothetical scenario serves to illustrate the impact when you start looking at the big picture and the aggregate numbers. Just think – a mere 10% improvement in this productivity drain equates to having 5 "lost" employees back firing on all cylinders every day of the month.

It is probably safe to say that as we go higher up in the organization, the execution of meetings becomes more focussed, and the engagement and productivity of the participants becomes a lot higher. However, it's the lower and middle levels where the cumulative un-productive meeting effect is probably the most prevalent.

When you start digging deeper and looking at large-number effects, other worrying statistics appear. For example, let's say the average time delay to the start of a meeting is 10 minutes. (I read online somewhere that it is just under 11 minutes).

So, using our same hypothetical meeting room scenario, we have:

40 rooms x 70% usage x 1 hr/meeting x

8 hrs/day =

224 meetings a day

If we have an average of 5 people in each meeting, and there are just 10 minutes average delay to the start, meaning the 5 participants have all wasted that time, then the number of employee hours wasted in a day just from a 10-minute delay to each meeting = **187 employee-hours per day!**

That's **23 employee-days lost per day** in the building, or over **500 employee-days per month**, just because of an average delay of 10 minutes to the start of each meeting, be it a face to face or a video meeting. Shocking, and again, calculated simply on the usage of the meeting rooms, and not on the number of employees.

And let's not forget the time it takes you to get to and from the meeting room, or the time you connect via video before the meeting starts, or the wait for the room to become available (as we all like to get there a few minutes early, don't we?). It all adds up.

Again, you can dispute the numbers, but I hope you get the idea. The loss of aggregated productivity when you look at the big picture, just considering time/resources due the multitude of meetings we hold, can be enormous.

Before going on, here's an alternative and equally quick way to have an idea of how much wastage your meetings might be causing.

From the statistics, a reasonable estimate for how much time on average a mid-level employee will be spending in meetings during a typical week is 20-25%. Obviously, this depends enormously on the nature of your business, and yes, the higher you go up the organization, this number increases significantly. But let's use this 20-25% as a good range.

Considering our 60% productivity factor as reasonable for any meeting, applicable to all participants, meaning 40% of the time the participants are being under-productive. We'll disregard the additional factors such as late starts, getting to the meeting or logging on and waiting for all the video participants to be connected.

Now multiply this estimated average total employee time spent in meetings (20-25%) by the under-productive estimate (40%) to get a "Meeting Productivity Loss" range of 0.08 – 0.1.

So that means some *8-10% of your workforce is probably being significantly under-productive all day every day simply due to their participation in meetings.*

So, if you have 200 people in your department or company, it implies that the equivalent of 16-20 employees being under-productive all day every day. 1000 employees in the company? That'll be 80-100 people all day every day!

Do it for yourself. How many meetings (hours) do you participate in during a typical week? What percentage of average productivity would you put on those meetings? Let's say 2 meetings a day, that's 10 hours a week, say 70% productive, that's 3 hours under-productive, which is almost 10% of your working week.

KEY POINT:	A mid-size to large organization which holds many meetings per day is probably suffering, as an absolute minimum, significant productivity deficiencies in some 8-10% of its workforce all day every day due to their meetings.

Quite dramatic and yes, you can argue the numbers. But it all points to the same thing. Lots of people and lots of meetings (physical or virtual) can create significant productivity losses, and this underpins the shocking losses in productivity of billions of dollars.

Let's make a quick estimation.

I Googled "How many meetings per day in the USA?". Eleven million came up. So, making a quick calculation:

11,000,000 x 5 people x 1 hour x 0,4% non-productive x 260 working days x USD30/hr

= USD 172 billion/year cost due to productivity deficiency

just on the 40% non-productive participation. Add on to that another **USD 72 billion losses** from the 10 minutes late start statistic and we're already up to almost **USD250 billion**.

Massive implications when you start looking at the global picture, and I repeat, you can argue all the numbers, but it all points to the same thing. Lots of meetings can add up to the effective "loss" of multiple employees all day every day.

Now, here's the paradox.

It's most likely you are thinking, "Yes, that's fine, but meetings are an essential part of the way we do our business, we can't do without them, and at our department level, this effect-of-scale doesn't apply, so we can live with it!".

That's seems a fair point. However, imagine if, every morning, a man comes into your office at precisely 9 o'clock and announces in a loud voice "How many people in this office? 100? Okay, I need 10 people to come with me and leave the building. They can have the day off!" And out troop the 10 employees. And that happens every working day!

I can guarantee you it would not take very long before someone (the manager) would be asking what's going on and try to put a stop to it.

Put differently, we all know how difficult it is a justify and get an extra employee, as headcount is one of the most closely scrutinised business indicators. So no, you can't hire another person...but you do accept having 10% of your staff under-productive all day, every day?

Hypothetical, perhaps, but it's probably very close to reality in most organizations that hold many meetings daily.

Anybody who convenes a meeting is usually convinced about the need to have that meeting. However, how much do they know about the **value perception** of the proposed meeting by the people they invite? This can also suffer a cumulative effect if the meetings are repetitive or periodic, like progress meetings, or weekly update meetings. What is the perceived, or even better, quantified, value for all?

Now, in the above discussion, I've focussed on the time and resource dedication aspects of meetings. However, non-productive meetings harbour several other insidious dangers. Let's have a look.

The Negative Aspects of Deficient Meetings

I have talked about productivity losses from poor meetings as being primordially time/resource based, meaning having employees being under-productive simply because of the time they are in meetings.

Good meetings produce great things - better decisions, agreements, motivation, team clarity, improved communication, alignment, team building, relationships, progress, transparency, and education. All positive aspects for a business environment.

But **deficiencies in any of the critical aspects** of a good meeting can generate significant downsides. Some effects will be short-term or spontaneous, others can have a more long-term effect.

Table 1 shows the most important aspects of a meeting. Each, done well (the left-hand column), contributes benefit and value both for the participants as well as the company. Done poorly (the right-hand column), the inverse is true.

The list is non-exhaustive, and there are probably other aspects you might consider important to include. However, the key aspects of a well-planned, well executed meeting produce tremendous benefit and value, whereas the downsides from deficiencies in any of these aspects can be extremely harmful. For example, one of the most important factors might be the last one – **validity**. A good meeting must be valid, or have meaning, for all the participants.

KEY POINT:	The negative effects of deficient or poorly executed meetings are not just about time being wasted. They can affect such issues as the quality of decisions and solutions, employee motivation, leadership and commitment and team performance.

GOOD MEETINGS	ASPECT	POOR MEETINGS
Clarity for all participants prior to the meeting as well as during the execution creates meaning, participation and buy-in	Objectives / Agenda / Process	Loss of interest, confusion, frustrations and poor or wrong outputs
Use rigorous and efficient decision-making techniques, leading to better decisions with buy-in from all participants	Decision making	Lead to lower quality decisions or decisions with less buy-in which can lead to problems further on
Use established and efficient problem analysis and solving techniques leading to better solutions with buy-in from all participants	Problem Solving	Can lead to wrong or partial solutions which can have important implications in the future
Motivate people and enhance employee loyalty and commitment	Motivation	Lead to a decline in employee motivation and commitment
Will contribute to the development of participants through peer-learning	Employee Development	Cause disenchantment and negatively affect employees
Are the backbone of a successful team	Team Building / Integration	Can destroy a team or cause it to under-perform.

Table 1 – Critical Aspects of Meetings

25

GOOD MEETINGS	ASPECT	POOR MEETINGS
Are the backbone of a successful team	**Team Building / Integration**	Can destroy a team or cause it to under-perform.
Can help to ensure good outcomes for all parties involved (win-win)	**Negotiations**	Can lead to poor results and non-sustainable outcomes (win-lose)
Pass the correct messages clearly and concisely	**Communication / Messaging**	Can lead to confusion or incorrect messages
Enhance the company's culture and identity	**Discipline / Culture / Behaviour**	Create a poor impression of the company's culture and lead to disenchantment, lack of rigour and/or disruption
Underline and enhance good leaders and leadership	**Leadership**	Can destroy or seriously undermine a leader or manager.
Have the correct information, the participants will have had timely access to any pre-reading material, and the presentation and sharing of information in the meetings will be optimal	**Information**	Have deficiencies in the availability, sharing, communication, pre-read and audiovisual presentations
Will be planned in advance, will be convenient for all participants and above all will have meaning for all participants	**Planning / Validity**	Can cause schedule conflicts, lack of commitment of participants, absenteeism

Table 1 (contd.) – Critical Aspects of Meetings

The Fried Egg Analogy

Here's a popular question. "How many types of meetings are there?"

Ask Google and you'll get answers running from 5 up to as many as 25. There are many websites offering a variety of classifications and theories on types of meetings, many backed up by very deep and thorough psychological theory and research. They are all valid and with their individual merits, and you can perhaps try to make your own list based on your own organization or way of working.

However, my proposal, and which is the basic tenet of this book, comes from looking at the things from a completely different perspective - by considering, quite simply, what meetings provide to the organization in terms of benefit and value.

To illustrate, I created what I call the **FRIED EGG ANALOGY.** Consider the following image

You will see there are three concentric circles. The outside of the PAN, the WHITE of the egg and the YOLK. These in turn provide three areas.

- *PAN - The black area between the pan edge and the white of the egg*

- *WHITE - The area of the white of the egg*

- *YOLK - The yellow area of the yolk of the egg*

Let's now think in terms of **nutritional value** in terms of food. The different areas offer different nutritional value.

> *PAN - Large area but holds zero nutritional value*

> *WHITE - Large area and provides some nutritional value*

> *YOLK - Smallest area but with the most nutritional value*

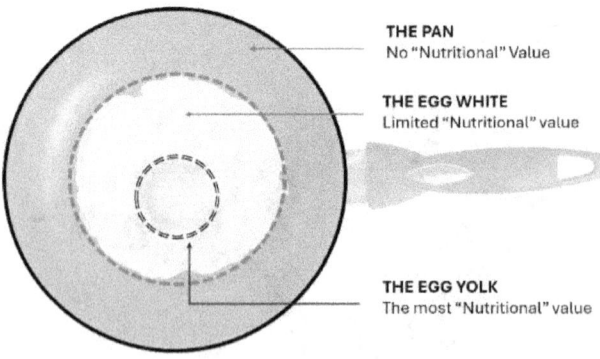

THE PAN
No "Nutritional" Value

THE EGG WHITE
Limited "Nutritional" value

THE EGG YOLK
The most "Nutritional" value

Now let's consider the different areas in terms of "nutritional" or intellectual value to the company, where the areas represent our meetings.

PAN - *Meetings which provide zero "nutritional" value for the company.*

WHITE - *Meetings which provide limited "nutritional" value.*

YOLK - *Meetings which provide the most "nutritional" value for the company.*

Expanding the analogy:

The PAN - represents all those meetings we hold which are **Unnecessary**. They not only provide zero nutritional value to the company and the participants, but often imply real negative value. Far more lost productivity that benefit. **These meetings need to be eliminated.**

The WHITE – meetings which provide some nutritional value, and most likely most of our meetings fall in this category. These meetings are necessary but do have deficiencies in terms of productivity, efficiency and/or results. **They need improving, with some even being eliminated.**

The YOLK - represent the star meetings. Those meetings which are most definitely necessary, have a high level of productivity, efficiency and benefit for all participants and provide maximum nutritional value to the company. **These are how we want all our meetings to be.**

It's a very simple analogy, but well describes the situation and the opportunity. And don't forget that when I talk about **nutritional value**, it's not just about time and resource involvement, but all those critical value-adding aspects of meetings.

Now consider the relative size of the three areas.

The YOLK is by far the smallest, with the PAN and the WHITE both much larger. This is probably a faithful representation of the meetings we hold. The number of perfect, high-value (YOLK) meetings is probably vastly inferior to those that either don't need to take place (PAN), or the majority of our meetings (WHITE) which have inherent inefficiencies/deficiencies, and which can be either eliminated or improved.

There is one other part of the image I have not mentioned, and that's the **Pan handle**.

This also has a part in the analogy, as it represents the means of control the Cook has over the cooking process.

It is essential for the Cook to hold the pan to manage the cooking, occasionally, or all the time. At one or more moments in the whole cooking process, the Cook holds the pan.

In our analogy, representing the hundreds, perhaps thousands, of employee-hours being spent in meetings, who is holding that handle and ensuring the best recipe and overall result? Probably no-one.

In the analogy, the Cook is quite simply Management.

We'll come back to the Fried Egg Analogy later, but at this point, I'm now going to pose another question.

Why is it that we don't bother evaluating our meeting culture?

Why Don't We Evaluate Our Meeting Culture?

Quite simply? Because we're all too busy and it isn't seen as a priority issue.

Ask anyone in a supervisory or management role in a company about their meeting culture, meeting efficiency and general "meeting health" and most will probably admit they are not all as good as they could be and "perhaps, yes, we probably do have too many".

Most will also argue that meetings are a necessary part of the business, and that in the aggregate, all the good that comes out of meetings far outweighs the bad. In other words, we certainly can't live without meetings, and yes, we can live with the way things are.

If we go further and ask managers or executives if they have ever evaluated or quantified the effectivity/productivity of their workforce's meeting culture, the most likely response will be along the lines of "No, and admittedly we probably could do better, but we have far more important things to do running the business!".

Everyone is too busy working on the "business" and there really is no time, nor is it a priority, to spend any resources or effort on trying to change things regarding meetings, beyond the odd set of simple guidelines sent out occasionally, such as "*No meetings after 16:30*", or "*Make sure you give plenty of advance warning to invitees*", or generic guidelines on agendas and objectives, which is where most of the meeting improvement literature and help focusses.

Now it's fair to say that the latest collaborative platforms have streamlined a lot of processes and made things more efficient, but meetings are still meetings.

I suspect many companies are, on the face of it, satisfied with their meeting culture because they have adopted one of these platforms, perhaps the most popular being MS-Teams. But while things might be easier and more fluid to manage in terms of process, does it necessarily mean we are more efficient in time/resource usage and productivity?

I mentioned before that that one of the most critical and constrained indicators of business is headcount. How often do we need, or think we need, additional resources to get that project through on time, but budgetary or HR constraints simply do not permit it?

So, what happens? Timeline over-runs, pressure-working, late nights, more stress on the team and hurried deliverables, which can often imply deficient outputs.

We saw in the previous chapter the enormous implications on time/resources caused by everyday meetings, where I proposed a very simple rule-of-thumb loss of productivity factor due to meetings of 8-10%, meaning you are probably accepting having 8-10% of your workforce significantly under-productive all day every day. That's a lot and is also probably considerably under-estimated.

If you're in a meeting where you are not particularly engaged (and this is particularly true with Videoconferencing) you will probably "multi-task", meaning that while you keep one ear on the meeting proceedings, you get on with some other stuff in parallel which is more pressing for you.

That does affect your own productivity when you consider the impact on yourself of having to participate in a meeting which was of little value to yourself. It will have reduced the time you could have spent on your important things.

Add this effect over several meetings and it'll probably sum up to several hours of affected time, which then put you under pressure to finish your more important tasks.

And that is just considering yourself. When you then consider a similar effect on a whole organization, it aggregates to a very large opportunity.

I'll mention again the collaborative IT platforms. They potentially bring many benefits, streamlining processes and creating that team-working environment, but can also mask over the problem, whereby we think by using such a platform we are doing much better. But do we really know?

So, to sum up, we know meetings are necessary, we know meetings produce good things for the company, but do we know what is the aggregate quantified picture for our company?

Have we quantified the number of resources involved on a day-to-day basis, their productivity, the efficiencies, and better still, the opportunities for improvement? The key word here is "quantified".

If you don't ask these sorts of question and make the occasional health check on how things are going, you will simply be accepting that, all day, every day, and probably as a minimum, at least 10% of your people are being under-productive at best, or completely non-productive. My proposal is that it is worth having a look.

Let's go back to the Fried Egg Analogy for a moment. The "PAN" meetings - those that are numerous and provide zero or negative value to the company. What should do we do with these? Quite simply eliminate them. However, in most cases that is easier said than done in a sustainable way. Solutions will probably mean re-visiting some of your work-flow processes, communication channels and information management.

As for the "WHITE" meetings, many could most likely be eliminated in the same way as the "PAN" meetings, and those that are essential need improvement to transform them into the excellent, high value "YOLK" type of meeting. Again, not a simple exercise and needs careful consideration.

The problem then is how can we know if we have a problem – or opportunity – and what to do about it?

The Quick Health Check

It is likely that most managers or executives will not put the consideration, let alone analysis, of the meeting culture of their department or organization high on the priority list, claiming "There is no time, resources or budget for such matters". Understandable and common.

This is also complicated by the remote working and videoconferencing culture. As remote working often implies a considerable amount of video participation, it is easy to take the position that "we have to have video conferences, so there is nothing we can do".

Also (and this is my own opinion here) remote working by its nature probably has increased the number of video meetings beyond the absolute necessary due to the remote worker feeling the need to frequently "connect" and be part of the organization.

Go back to the Fried Egg Analogy. Meetings, no matter if they are presential, virtual of hybrid still fall into one of the three areas – the PAN, the WHITE or the YOLK.

So, my proposal is to simply start by asking a few questions in the simplest, most resource-efficient and cost-effective way to get an indication of whether there may be an opportunity.

How do we do this? Well, there is no one solution for all, and much would depend on the nature of your business and the nature of the way you conduct business. Are we purely a face-to-face organization, do we have occasional remote participation or are we mainly video? Whichever, careful thought needs to be given to how we are operating before asking any questions.

It also depends on who you are. Are you an executive with part of, or even the whole company in your hands, or are you in a management position with employees under your supervision, or are you simply and employee in a team?

Obviously if you are in charge, it is much more straightforward to implement any kind you action you see fit. If you're not in charge, it's more challenging.

The key here is to accept that yes, it is worth asking the question and getting some real, meaningful feedback and information **with as little effort and interference as possible to the day-to-day**. This will serve as an indicator as to whether there is an opportunity.

Let's assume you are in charge. One approach could be to design, over a short-term period and with an appropriate scope of employees, departments or business areas, a simple survey or data collection protocol. With the objective of causing as little extra work as possible for everyone, a simple one-shot survey, or over a period, can be implemented either as a bespoke design perhaps by the IT department, or any other simple methodology (for example, there are many off-the-shelf survey apps around for such purposes).

If, however, you are not in charge, then there are other ways you could approach the problem. For example, either by yourself, or with the cooperation of a few colleagues, start compiling some statistics over say a month, of such things as:

- How many meetings do I have per month
- What percentage of my time
- My estimate of average productivity for myself
- Average Delay time
- Quality of meeting ratings

Once you have a set of data, you can use this to persuade your manager that you think there are some opportunities.

The simplest of meeting surveys could even be using the Fried Egg classification. Maybe have all your employees in your sample rate your meetings (all participants of all meetings) over a month as BLACK (Pan), WHITE or YELLOW (Yolk). You'd obviously need to list a few criteria to clearly describe what constitutes what in the three categories.

Whatever your initial "test the water" survey, the old adage really does stand true. "If you don't measure it, you don't know!" and no more so than regarding the hundreds of employee-hours spent in meetings.

So, my recommendation, and perhaps the most important takeaway from this book, is to **make the commitment to undertake a quick health-check validated by data.** And that commitment requires spending some thought on the design of such a health check to ensure the most valuable and useable feedback in the most effective and efficient manner, no matter how simple or in-depth you want it to be.

> **KEY POINT:** Don't assume everything is as good as it can be. Make a quick quantified health check to see if there are any opportunities.

This data-based feedback should then indicate if there is an opportunity and where it might lie. You might be pleasantly surprised, finding your employees or colleagues are perfectly happy with the way things are, and you continue without changing anything. That is great, but the key is you have asked the question, you have checked, and you know!

> **KEY POINT:** An initial investigation should be as simple and efficient as possible to provide meaningful feedback but with minimal disturbance to the organization.

It is more likely, however, after a quick feeling of the pulse via a survey period, some things will stand out as possible opportunities, and it is important as with any improvement initiative, to then *evaluate the implications, the costs and the overall benefits of trying to change things.* This might involve taking the analysis to another level, expanding the scope or going straight to the design of corrective measures.

It is important to try to quantify the implications of the findings in terms of productivity, numbers, resources and ultimately cost, as that is what it is all about. As we all know, once issues are put into monetary value, attention automatically becomes a lot more focussed.

One thing I do know, having been involved in many change initiatives in my career, there is no doubt that "small is beautiful", and starting with a smaller, easier scope, then expanding on proven and publicised success is far easier than trying to "go big" from the outset. However, the approach would depend entirely on executive decision, commitment, sponsorship and involvement.

Also, the question arises about who's responsibility is this? Who is holding the pan's handle? If I were to hazard a guess, based on the twenty-first century culture of most companies, as meetings are seen as "People" events and employee practices, it would most probably be assumed it's a Human Resources issue.

A considerable amount of business responsibility has moved onto the HR departments' desk over the years, which were once very much the remit of general management.

In my opinion, this issue of meetings is one that should be under the leadership of operational management, as many aspects of the business are involved, such as inter-departmental interaction, document and information management, collaboration, communication, process, systems and the like. However, each organization would have its own preference as to how to tackle this issue.

> **KEY POINT:** Before trying to implement change, evaluate fully the implications in terms of effort/cost versus benefit.

What Next?

So maybe you've reflected and thought, yes, we do have lots of meetings, presential, virtual and hybrid, and you've made a quick check via a survey or collecting some data, the result of which shows some opportunities for improvement.

This basic information has then been extrapolated into potential benefit in terms of productivity, resource efficiency, quality of outputs which indicate considerable benefit for the organization. So, let's do something about it and stop those 10% of people leaving the office every day.

If shown to be potentially significant, the opportunity should be taken seriously and put up there in the priority list for either (a) further investigation/analysis/evaluation or (b) direct action to tackle the issues and look for solutions.

At this point, either for (a) or (b), it is important to formalise things under rigorous project management/change initiative principles.

In my experience, there will be some obvious quick fixes, the low-hanging fruit, and whilst giving an immediate positive feedback and positive impression to the organization, the quick fixes tend to relatively superficial and more than likely will not last very long.

When you think about it, meetings involve, affect, or are affected by:

- People
- Communication channels and methodologies
- Information
- Logistics
- Systems
- Processes
- Protocols
- Needs
- Cultures

But whatever you include in this list, what is evident is that what's driving your meeting culture can be a complex interaction of all these elements.

Long-lasting and deep-rooted solutions (for the PAN and WHITE meetings) need to be very well investigated, analysed, mapped, quantified, implemented and measured because they affect, or are affected by a multitude of considerations.

Every department or organization would have its own requirements and methodologies, but a standard project management approach is recommended for well-designed solutions to well analysed problems. So, you'll probably want to go along these lines:

1) Make a quick health check, and quantification of possible benefits.

2) Decision gate –>

   a. yes, we want to take this seriously, CONTINUE

   b. or no we're happy as we are or there is no apparent cost-benefit advantage beyond a few quick fixes - END

If you decide, after an initial quantification of potential benefit, that there is value in going further, it should be approached with objectives, timeline, scoping, budget, resources etc.

- Design and implementation of further data collection (if needed)
- Analysis, evaluation and benefit quantification
- Solution(s) design
- Implementation
- Monitoring

I will not go any further regarding possible approaches to analysis, evaluation and design of solutions as every organization is different and would probably have different aspirations, possibilities and needs.

Suffice to say that I really do recommend a multi-disciplinary approach due to the many aspects, interactions, processes and systems which make up your meeting culture.

There is an enormous amount of publicised material available for meeting improvement of those WHITE meetings, mainly focussed on the execution of the meeting, as well as how to plan and program better.

But let's consider for a moment those "PAN" meetings. Zero or negative value meetings, which basically need to be eliminated. A simple (and common) internal communication stating "*Please try to reduce the number of meetings and only hold those that are really necessary*" will probably make very little difference.

You need to look at the underlying reasons why people are having these unnecessary meetings and what needs to be done as long-term, water-tight solutions and processes to ensure they are not only eliminated, but do not start to come back. Root cause analysis is a wonderful thing!

So yes, solutions for the "PAN" and "WHITE" areas will probably involve addressing the underlying processes, systems, communication and information-sharing aspects of business, whilst focus on the planning and execution of the "WHITE" meetings will move them towards the excellence of the "YOLK" meetings.

I'm now going to move on to the second biggest message of this book. The first was to not underestimate the importance in terms of productivity of your meeting culture and overlook the potential opportunities and benefits that may lie therein. You really should to evaluate it.

The second message is regarding the "WHITE" and the "YOLK" meetings. As said, there is a massive amount of information and literature available on how to improve the execution of a meeting, through better agendas, objectives and the like.

However, it is not the purpose of this book to get into that. What I will mention though, is what I believe to be *one of the most under-rated, and under-used tools that can vastly improve the execution of a meeting, and that is the use of independent facilitation.*

Facilitation

Facilitation is, in my opinion the single biggest missed opportunity in the world of meeting culture and improvement.

Meetings commonly have leaders, will have organisers, but independent facilitation is rarely used on a day-to-day basis. Why is this?

Let's first look at what a facilitator is. Here are a few definitions pulled off the Internet.

> ***"A person (or thing) that makes an action or process easy or easier"***

> ***"Someone who helps to bring about an outcome (such as learning, productivity, or communication) by providing indirect or unobtrusive assistance, guidance, or supervision".***

> ***"A facilitator acts as a neutral third-party, encouraging participation, managing conflicts, and drawing out collective intelligence from the group".***

This last one I particularly like, because it specifically mentions four key value-adders of facilitation, even though there are several other key functions not mentioned in this definition and which we will address later.

Let's look at those four in more detail.

1) ***A Facilitator is a neutral third-party*** - meaning they have little or no direct stake in the objectives or outcome of the meeting beyond making it a success. They

don't have, or take, a position on the issues under discussion. This allows them to focus on the dynamics and process of the meeting.

2) *A Facilitator encourages participation* – thereby directly increasing the productivity of each participant and consequently, that of the whole group.

3) *A Facilitator manages conflicts* – and eliminates disruptive and non-productive aspects, producing better decisions and solutions, and more buy-in from the participants.

4) *A Facilitator draws out collective intelligence* – using techniques which allow the group to all contribute to the design of optimal outcomes, which are usually better than a single individual's proposal.

Expanding on these four key functions, a meeting facilitator specifically enforces and imposes other value-adding "process" aspects of a good meeting, such as

- Helping the participants in achieving the meeting objective(s)
- Enforcing the ground rules, discipline and behaviour.
- Keeping track of time and progress and agenda compliance.
- Being aware of the dynamics of each participant and the collective group.
- Ensuring 100% engagement from all the participants.
- Extinguishing/avoiding those negative aspects of meetings

- Guides the participants in the use of collective thinking tools (Root Cause Analysis, Problem Solving etc).
- Keeping a level playing field

Another way to look at it is by reminding ourselves of the most common destructive aspects to a meetings success.

- Poor planning/ scheduling (including late invites, schedule-conflicts)
- Dominant or disruptive participants
- Too short a time for the necessary actions/decisions
- Deficient information sharing or availability
- Wrong/missing participants
- Monologues or story telling
- Hierarchy
- Culture mismatches
- Facilities

A good facilitator knows how to deal with all these issues and keeps the meeting on track to comply with its objectives and more importantly ensure maximum value for each participant and the collective outcome for the company.

So why are facilitators not used more often in day-to-day, routine meetings? I believe for the following reasons:

a) Most people, especially supervisors, managers and executives do not understand or recognise the value of an independent facilitator and, if they are organising or leading their own meeting, they are convinced that they can lead the meeting perfectly well themselves. Leading a meeting (as an active participant) and facilitating a meeting are entirely different, especially if you are leading from a position of authority.

b) Facilitators are generally considered experts, with certification and training, and are therefore an expensive luxury, only to be used for major events – such as workshops - where the cost can be justified.

c) A facilitator is perceived as an additional a resource with a Time/Cost aspect and everyone is too busy. No one has time to act as a facilitator.

d) Organizations generally do not have a Facilitator resource pool, acting as a service outfit for use by the entire organization.

e) Very few employees are trained, or have any experience, in facilitation techniques.

f) A Facilitator removes the "advantage" of a participant or party of the group.

Let me comment on each of these five aspects.

The first one, (a), is perhaps the most important. Every meeting has an organiser and a leader. Someone who is running the meeting. As professionals move up the ladder into more senior positions, they become more experienced, generally more confident and self-assured, and become "leaders". They know how things should be done. They have authority.

So, when a supervisor or manager, or even less-senior employees organises a meeting, they have the self-confidence to run it, but *generally their focus is on their own objectives*. And this is the key. Nobody organises a meeting, which they themselves will lead, without thinking through the dynamics, the participants and have clear in their mind what they want out of it. They invite people to participate, they create discussion, they lead the meeting, but generally with their own objectives very much in mind.

A facilitator does not suffer from this "need to lead" position. They have no opinion on the outcome as such, and they don't have the pieces of knowledge that come from the participants. What they do is ensure that all the participants are equal, that they all have the right – and are given the opportunity – to speak and will promote the auto-critique of decisions and draw out the collective power of the group.

Here is a common occurrence. A meeting will be convened, and, at the last minute, a particular representative might be invited. "*Oh, we need someone from accounting there...*" so the invite is sent out, and the unfortunate accounting person is duly sent along to sit there at the back, get through it and leave without rocking the boat.

The facilitator, however, will oblige that participant to present an opinion from the accounting department, ensuring the others get at least an opinion from someone from accounts. Also, the accounts representative will have to become engaged if it is stated (as the facilitator should) at the beginning that everyone is aware who is present and why and that all are expected to participate.

So, leaders consider they have the experience and quite simply the leadership qualities to run the show but will be focussed on achieving their own objectives. A facilitator on the other hand, ensures that the group of people participate, question, think, discuss and above all *collectively* produce results respecting an agenda, objectives and a time frame.

The second and third reasons (b) and (c), why Facilitation is not used more often, is that Facilitators are considered experts, with certification and training, and are therefore expensive and only used for major events, not for day-to-day business.

In my opinion, this is a major misconception and failing and goes hand-in-hand with points (d) and (e); few people know how to facilitate a meeting and there is normally no pool of people available for facilitation.

Yes, there are seasoned, certified professional facilitators out there with years of experience, but the basics of facilitation are relatively easily learned. Not only is it not particularly difficult, but it is also enormously motivating and serves as a phenomenal training ground for people-management skills.

I recommend that everyone at every level should have some facilitation training, especially as it really does focus on two key core competencies – ***listening and process!***

With the minimum of training, employees of all levels can act as a facilitator for meetings of virtually any level, and vastly improve the quality and efficiency of those meetings.

Obviously, experience of facilitation will enhance competency, in the same way that seniority and experience enhance self-confidence to lead. I certainly wouldn't propose a junior employee with a minimum of experience to facilitate a board meeting!

Finally, point (e), that a Facilitator eliminates advantage. One key role of a facilitator is to maintain a level playing field and remove advantage from any one participant or group. The easiest illustration is that of the boss. Simply because of his/her hierarchical authority, the boss usually has an advantage in the proceedings. A facilitator can reduce or even eliminate this advantage allowing a much more open discussion.

KEY POINT:	**Facilitation should not be a "luxury" only for workshops and meetings. Basic facilitation can increase significantly the output value of any meeting, and facilitation training is an enormously valuable people-management skill.**

My proposal, therefore, is that the competency of facilitation should be instilled in every employee from an early age and developed throughout their careers.

It improves leadership qualities and develops self-confidence, but also will lead to better decision making and problem-solving skills, better negotiation abilities and perhaps most important of all, ***better listening skills.*** Because that is what a Facilitator is doing most during a meeting - listening, as well as observing and prodding and guiding and suggesting.

Maybe every employee could be given a target to facilitate a certain number of meetings in a given time period and post their availability to join anyone's meeting – from any department, their own or others - as a facilitator. It's a great experience, it makes meetings so much more productive and doesn't need to be considered as something extraordinary. It should be ordinary.

Now – a word of warning here. The best facilitator in the world will not make a success out of a poorly planned or organised meeting! In other words, the more the important or complex the meeting, the more important it is that the facilitator (i) be experienced and (ii) be involved in the design of the meeting, going through the dynamics and the processes – and hence the agenda – well in advance.

On this last point, a facilitator should always have prior knowledge of the objectives, the agenda and the participants of a meeting he/she is to facilitate.

> **KEY POINT:** **The best facilitator in the world will not make a success out of a poorly planned or organised meeting!**

I will not go into the specifics of a Facilitators toolbox or training. That is outside the scope of this book. However, should you wish to know more, please visit my website (www.sjfacilitation.com).

Neither am I proposing a facilitator for every meeting you hold, because yes, a Facilitator is a resource with associated cost.

However, just go back and do the maths. Large numbers of meetings cause a significant number of resources being under-productive all day every day, so even the smallest improvement in productivity, which a facilitator can bring, can offer real positive value.

And that includes the intangible benefits of a great meeting which facilitation brings and which should not be under-estimated. Like the enjoyment and feel-good factor of the meeting, the increase in team-cohesion, the feeling of efficiency in problem solving or decision making, the quality of the outputs, the buy-in, the engagement, and the self-development of all participants (including the facilitator) on how better to manage teams.

So, if not all meetings need facilitation, which ones do? I would say that, as a rule of thumb, for any meeting which involves

- Complex issues
- Several issues to discuss
- More than 5 people
- A lot of discussion is expected
- Negotiations or conflict resolution
- Problem analysis or solving
- Decision making
- Contentious or confrontational issues
- Cultural issues

even the most basic of facilitation would improve the experience and the outcomes.

Now, facilitating a video conference or a hybrid meeting presents a slightly different set of challenges regarding facilitation compared to purely face-to-face meetings.

In face-to-face meetings, body language is a massive contributor to both the other participants and to the observant facilitator. However, pretty much all body-language is lost in videoconferencing, as is the collective "being in the same room" feeling.

That said, facilitation is as valid in a video conference or a hybrid meeting as in a face-to-face meeting, but the skills, awareness and techniques required are slightly different.

As an example, in a face-to-face meeting, a good facilitator should never sit at the table together with the meeting participants. He/she walks around, avoiding as much as possible being always at front and centre stage, otherwise the participants tend to talk directly to the facilitator instead of discussing between themselves, and the meeting becomes the facilitators meeting. This shouldn't happen.

Now, to do this in a video conference isn't possible. The facilitator is shown on a screen like any other participant, so their speech, and the rules and the dynamics and techniques are different. They are effectively "sat at the table" like any of the other participants.

It is more difficult, but as said before, with a minimal amount of basic training, anyone can facilitate and improve the dynamics and output of a video or hybrid meeting. One trick is to eliminate visual image of the facilitator in the Videoconference, simply acting as the overseer, or "voice" behind the scenes.

A final comment on facilitation for the reader who does not work in a large company, and who's working "environment" has relatively fewer meetings.

The benefits of facilitation equally apply, but perhaps accessing the facilitator as a resource is probably a lot more restrictive. My suggestion would be to have a training session for your team on facilitation, as having been exposed to the techniques does help every single participant be more aware of how a meeting can be improved, and for the occasional more complex or important meeting, make a trial.

You'll probably find that the increase in value of the meeting, both in time, productivity and value to all, will increase the perceived value of a facilitator to the point where even for your small business, the occasional use is valid from a cost/resource point of view.

You can even pick someone in your organization – preferably a volunteer – to take on the role as a more accepted and permanent part of their job.

Training

Recognising that being in meetings uses up a significant amount of every employee's working day, and collective team-based activities are more and more common, how much training does the average employee get on meetings? Like planning, preparing, attending or running a meeting, to ensure the best possible outcome for all involved, both individually and as a group?

In my experience and talking to folks, the answer is generally none! In almost 40 years, I never had any training at all regarding meetings.

Problem Solving techniques in groups, Prioritization techniques, Root Cause Analysis, Brainstorming, and Decision making. These are all important components of meetings, and to undertake these tasks in groups involves different and well-established tools and techniques. Employees should know about these techniques and be well versed in their usage.

Just think about the characters and personalities you have in your department, or company. A complete range, I am sure, and just by putting all these different folks around a table together and presuming that their understanding of how to behave and participate and get the best out of the group is common knowledge and understood by all, is a very tall order.

For example, the confident, talkative, assertive person, or perhaps the boss, should be aware of their perceived "character" strength in a meeting compared to say, the quiet, reserved person and vice versa. Do we ever go through any awareness training from a personal "reflection" perspective for meeting participation? Probably not.

Note the word "Awareness". This is probably one of the most important words for a successful meeting culture. Awareness of the needs, the objectives, the personalities, the surroundings, the progress, the tensions, the dynamics, the needs of the individuals and the meeting as a collective entity.

I mentioned earlier that I have been in many a meeting where it was obvious that the objective of one or more participants was to out-shine everybody else, and self-promote themselves - and let's face it, meetings are a showcase for your talents, like it or not!

Whilst this is always going to happen, training in meeting behaviour and protocols – and awareness – can turn this into a benefit for all.

Meeting "culture" is complex enough within the walls of your own department or organization. When we expand to include meetings with third parties, other cultures, other corporate methodologies and preferences, different languages, and the whole thing becomes massively exposed to a multitude of potential deficiencies. And this brings me back to the need for facilitation.

All companies implement training programs for those issues deemed important – technical and non-technical. Some are specialised by competency or by hierarchy. So why not on how to get the best out of running, or being part of a meeting, knowing that it is where so much time is spent, so much time is lost and the outcomes of which can be crucial for the performance of the business?

Wrap-Up

As with any good meeting, an adequate amount of time needs to be left at the end for the closure - and yes, this tends to be one of the most common deficiencies of those WHITE meetings. Poor closure.

As I said at the beginning, the purpose of this book is not to provide any specific solution to the deficiencies of a company's meeting culture, but to convince the reader that the issue of meetings may be an important source of an opportunity to improve productivity and warrants taking a look.

That said, let's go through my key messages.

1) Meetings are an essential component of business and always will be. Whilst a lot of good comes out of meetings, we have seen that the un-productive aspects can cause considerable downsides for an organization.

2) When you start to aggregate all the meetings and employee hours involved daily in an organization and the cost associated to those hours, the numbers add up very quickly.

3) "Losses" from poor meetings are not limited to time. They also affect quality of outputs, motivation, team health, sustainable decisions and buy-in.

4) Every person probably thinks about meetings from their own individual viewpoint and how the meetings they have affect just themselves. But who is looking at the big picture?

5) If you organise a lot of meetings because of your role in the organization and the nature of your job, you will probably be more self-assured about the positive value of those meetings. However, what do other people think?

6) Companies tend to recognize that all is not perfect with their meeting culture but consider it as a necessary burden to doing business and is certainly not a priority issue. Looking at publicised statistics, this is a very blasé assumption when headcount and productivity mean so much and are so key to optimizing results.

7) There is absolutely no reason not to make a quick health check on your meeting culture. A quick, data-driven evaluation of an organization's situation, either on the small departmental scale or even companywide, through simple questionnaires, surveys, feedback and data can give a very good indication very quickly if there are any problems and therefore, opportunities.

8) Whilst there are many ways to categorize meetings, when considered in terms of creating or destroying value for a company, I propose there are only three, as illustrated by The Fried Egg Analogy. There are

   a. The PAN meetings - the zero or negative value meetings which should be eliminated,

   b. The WHITE meetings - probably the majority of meetings, which need improvement in productivity (with some perhaps being eliminated)

   c.   The YOLK Meetings - the necessary, excellent meetings to which all should aspire.

9) The PAN and the WHITE meetings are the majority and where the bigger opportunities lie. To treat the PAN and WHITE areas of the Fried Egg model, you need to go beyond the simple planning and execution aspects of meetings. The improvement solutions involve looking at processes, systems and protocols. Quick fixes rarely last.

10) Meeting culture is not just about good agendas, clear objectives and ground rules. It involves information management and sharing, collaboration, communication, planning, and processes.

11) The increase in videoconferencing and hybrid meetings, together with the incorporation of advanced collaborative platforms has changed the meeting landscape. However, it is dangerous to assume that the introduction of a particular collaborative platform increases your productivity and efficiency. It should be checked.

12) You can only know where you stand if you acquire data, even if some of that data is pure opinion (like for example the statistic regarding the number of employees feeling overwhelmed by the number of meetings they must attend).

13) If you are in a managerial role, you can make an evaluation happen. If you are not, you can collect data by yourself or

with a few colleagues to then take to your management to convince them.

14) If there is an indication of opportunity, it needs to be taken seriously and look for the root causes. Quick fixes rarely endure, and usually only scratch the surface.

15) Solid project management principles should be applied to any investigative or rectifying "change" initiatives.

16) The most under-valued and under-used "tool" for meeting improvement is the use of independent facilitation. Unfortunately, facilitation is seen as an extraordinary luxury rather than being a mainstream service. Making the competency and use of facilitation more widespread can bring extraordinary results.

17) Facilitation training/experience is an extremely valuable competence for all employees at all levels, and as a critical component of people management.

18) The problem isn't just in the large corporations. Every business environment involves meetings, and meetings mean people and people mean time, money, productivity and quality of outputs.

So, based on almost 40 years of being in every type of meeting you can imagine; I repeat the overall takeaway message. Do not ignore the elephant in the room and assume your meeting culture is adequate, or optimal, and doesn't need an occasional health check.

Remember those 10% of your employees that get marched out of the building every morning!

With the sheer numbers of meetings being held, and the number of people involved every working day, face-to-face or remotely, having any systemic inefficiencies or lack of productivity can be hugely detrimental to an organization when looking at the overall big picture. We suspect it, but we don't do anything about it.

So, if you are a manager, it's in your hands. Don't just assume it's OK and it's not worth bothering about. If you are lower on the ladder, you probably feel it most. Therefore, it's up to you to suggest to management, or find a way, using data, to convince them.

As you close this book, just think about your own meeting experiences in general terms. On a scale of 1 to 10, where would you put your average meeting "evaluation", considering time spent, productivity, enjoyment, motivation, and overall value?

If it's less than 10 and you have a lot of meetings, think about the collective implication of that for your department or organization, and think of the opportunity.

Next budget time, when you are haggling over the headcount and trying to get those extra employees approved, think about those 10% existing employees that effectively "leave" the office every morning due to the meetings they have to attend.

As a final comment, there seem to be so many more departments now in the larger organizations which did not exist in my day, such as Sustainability, Diversity and Inclusion, Governance, Employee well-being...the list goes on.

But, considering the amount of time the entire workforce spends in meetings, and the enormous implications those meetings have, nobody seems to be taking care of this issue as a specific area of focus.

Why do we not have a Meeting Improvement Group, which exclusively looks after our meeting culture? Which monitors progress and status through indicators, evaluates collaborative platforms, provides meeting training and provides a facilitation service for the organization? Such an entity could produce a seismic improvement in productivity, effectiveness and company identity and provide enormous *quantifiable* value to the company.

Great meetings not only boost productivity and improve outputs and results, but are a reflection on the professionalism, dynamism and quality of any organization.

So, with that, I hope some of the ideas presented here ring some bells, and I'll leave you with a few true-to-the-mark quotations on meetings. I do particularly like the last one!

Enjoy your meetings!

JF

www.sjfacilitation.com

Meeting Quotations

Meetings are by definition, a concession to a deficient organization. For one either meets or one works.

Peter Drucker

When the outcome of a meeting is to have another meeting, it has been a lousy meeting.

Herbert Hoover

Meetings are a symptom of bad organization. The fewer meetings the better.

Peter Drucker

The longer the meeting, the less is accomplished.

Tim Cook

Approach every meeting with a purposeful, high-energy, ready-to-make-a-contribution attitude, and watch how fast leadership's perception of you follows your behaviour.

Jack Welch

It has to be an awfully good meeting to beat having no meeting at all.

Boyd K. Packer

The usefulness of any meeting is inversely proportional to the size of the group.

Lane Kirkland

I've searched all the parks in all the cities - and found no statues of Committees.

Gilbert K. Chesterton